All of

A Collection

L.M. Giannone

Copyright

ISBN: 978-1-365-64556-3 (paperback)

Printed by Lulu Independent Publishing
FIRST EDITION

Dedication

For Ben, today and always...

Table of Contents

Poems

Fade

What light was left has faded altogether
ushering in a darkness so encompassing
a nothingness so unbearable
a world so cold
without the warmth of your sun
come out from behind those gray clouds
shine your light on me again
before I fade away into oblivion

Reason

You are the reason I get up each morning
to rise and face the day
you are the reason I breathe
to aspire and to dream
there would be no cause
if you weren't here with me
may there always be a reason

When You're Gone

You were but a bud that once blossomed
now wilting in my hands
like a dried up, dead rose
in the morning when you're gone
all I'm left with is our stained bed
and memories of time gone by
and my heart on the floor
twisted and shattered

Not Me

I'm not who you think I am
was never whom you thought I was
I couldn't play the part
that you needed me to just because
I'm not one to be cornered
nor one to be tamed
won't ever be captured
on this pedestal I can't remain
I'm much too independent
unwilling to settle down
too much a free spirit
anything more I would drown
it pains me to hurt you
an illusion I can't be
some lucky woman will capture your heart
but that woman just isn't me
you fell in love with a shadow
in shades and hues unreal
I can't reciprocate actions or words
or feelings I just do not feel
you see me through a veil
blind to my imperfections and scars
looking through rose-coloured glasses
with your head too high in the stars
I will always be haunted
by the words I wouldn't say
you deserve so much better
out of love I couldn't stay
I know it hurts like hell
but in due time you'll heal
and you'll find someone else
who's worthy of you for real

When

How long will it be before my heart will beat again?
when will this blue blood stop coursing through my veins?
my arrhythmic pulse grows weary

When will I be able to hear a song,
read a passage,
or breathe without thinking of you?
wondering if you're okay,
if you miss me as much as I miss you?

When will I stop seeing you on busy sidewalks,
in stairwells,
on subways,
or in my dreams?

When will I be able to tune out your voice
echoing through the space between my ears?
when will your soul vacate my heart
allowing room for someone else?

Our conversations keep replaying in my head
like a record needle stuck in a worn-out groove
faint glimpses of a specter that won't stop haunting me
torturing and taunting me
memories that won't set me free
stopping me cold in my tracks

If I can still smell you,
taste you,
and touch you
then why do I still feel so numb?

Melancholia in C Minor

The C word.
No, not THAT "C" word.
The other one.
The one you think will never apply to you.
The one you think will never impact you.
The one you think you are immune to.
The one that happens to other people.
The one that's unthinkable.
The one that's incomprehensible.
The one that's ugly.
The one that's ruthless.
The one that changes your life.
The one that robs your dignity.
The one that zaps your strength.
The one that renders you powerless.
The one that claims life too soon.
The one that affects both men and women, young and old.
The one you pray you'll never hear from your doctor.
Until one day you do.

Flight of the Caged Bird

All that I am and all I can be
is because of you, you set me free
gifts you have given I can never repay
and now it's time to go my own way
saved me from drowning, loved me when lost,
healed my open wounds, now I must go at all costs
away from suffering, away from pain,
away from this pedestal on which I can't remain
open the door of this gilded cage
this bird was meant to fly, time to turn the page
I must spread my wings and soar across the sky
you always understood me and know not to ask why
now one last kiss before I go my own way
savour this final moment, then let me fly away

Visions

Visions float throughout my mind
feeling like a fool
falling ever far inside
the deep end of a pool
water washes over me
drowning in its depth
sinking to the bottom
'til none of me is left

Fragile

Pictures of you are all that remain
tears on my face trails of salty stain
like a weeping willow my branches scrape ground
I'm lost here without you so needing to be found
you turned off your light, I'm afraid of the dark
it's so cold without you, you made quite a mark
needing to hibernate and return to your shell
craving space and solitude, at least for a spell
introverted and loner, isolation you crave
away from the madding crowd for your sanity to save
had no idea how fragile you are
from your cocoon's safety pulled out too far
I wanted to help you, so damaged and broken
but you ran into hiding leaving so much unspoken
there's a void in my heart where you once occupied
for a moment my lifeline, now part of me's died
you have no idea how special you are
beauty inside and out in spite of deep scars
I shall never forget the gifts that you gave
with profound impact, it's me that you saved
we built quite a bond, a connection we shared
when and if you're ready, just know I'll be here

Bottle

Your punching bag in motion
doormat you walk across
disrespect me and yourself
you a product of your past
me a victim of your present
bottles of gin strewn across the floor
with stale, foul breath and glossy eyes
slurred speech and compromised mind
stumbling across the ruins of your life
your loss leads to my demise
pulling me down into your abyss
spiraling with centripetal force
mutual assured destruction

Kaleidoscope

Red and orange, green, yellow and blue
indigo and violet, a bit of every hue
illusion with mirrors, reflection of light
symmetrical patterns emerge and delight
like a kaleidoscope, your mood is erratic
first hot, then cold, so often sporadic
ambivalent and impulsive
unstable and indecisive
your capricious nature so well I know
personality which face will you show
turn the cylinder and change the view
to see a different side of you

Tidal Wave

Large waves crashing over me
pounding on the shore
drag me in their undertow
deafened by their roar
swimming in your ocean
intoxicated by your presence
spelunking through your caverns
drowning in your essence
quickly losing buoyancy
sinking out of view
water occupies my lungs
weighted by anchor of you
coastal winds picking up
I swim against the current
caught up in your riptide
my attraction growing fervent
drifting farther out to sea
away from safety's reach
wishing for a life line
or a rescue back to beach
it's futile to fight a tidal wave
its size is too immense
overwhelmed by your profound effect
my feelings are so intense
if we cannot be together
then release the ties that bind
and leave me lying on the shore
for another beachcomber to find

Oasis

Dunes shift as clouds of sand skip through the air
across this vast arid desert you're a welcoming oasis
your water beckons me to imbibe
and quench my insatiable thirst
drinking you in to the point of inebriation
planting my stake in this barren region
to tame your wilderness
worn down fighting a vortex
overheated with hungry desire
as we succumb to corporeal pleasures
two sets of footprints in the sand
no longer desolate or alone

When It's Love

It's something unmistakable, most assuredly inexplicable
taking hold and control over you
'til you're someone you don't recognize
all of a sudden you're selfless,
existing to please someone else
giving just because you want to,
expecting nothing in return
putting another's needs above your own
even if it's not in your best interest
willingly overlooking foibles, forgiving
accepting differences that make them unique
letting the other be right at least some of the time
absorbing another's pain
to protect them from harm or sadness
no matter how busy or how many conflicting demands
or how little sleep you got the night before
dropping everything to give it your all
even if it's just an ear or shoulder supporting them
helping their dreams come true
even if those dreams take them further away from you
making you a better person because of them
how do I know?
because I was in love once…

Strum

Wearing a smile while hurting inside
craving solitude you withdraw and hide
eyes full of passion now filled with sadness
your radiance dimmed surrounded by madness
like the tide of the ocean your mood ebbs and flows
victim of past demons and scars you only know
craving due solace with despair and pain
you play your guitar with a sad refrain
as you further retreat into your private hell
my own pain increases a state I know so well
while you strum your guitar my heart strings break
watching you suffer no end is difficult to take
your atonal melody modulated by change in chord
staccato notes can be softened when we work in accord
together we'll alter destiny a happier riff you will play
in my arms you'll know comfort, in my heart you'll stay

April Showers

Pitter patter on the roof
down the pipes and eaves
rain falling everywhere
drenching earth and leaves
in a gale or gust of wind
umbrella flipping out
water dripping down my face
now am soaked without
water pouring over me
cleansing sin and stain
remnants of an impure life
spiral down the drain
effecting transformation
erasing dirt and grime
emancipated from the past
clean slate reversing time
when the storm moves on
and gray clouds start to clear
the sun returns to the sky
rebirth now is here

Marionette

Standing back from these burning embers
ashes that once represented my life
once filled with blissful happiness
now pain cuts my soul like a knife
with a great big hole in my heart
a space where you once occupied
from grief of your loss
I've ached, mourned and cried
you wouldn't see it through
started but couldn't finish
re-opening fragile wounds
preventing pain to diminish
incessant, irresistible tease
so artfully come and go
lead me on then disappear
like tidal ebb and flow
only fantasies provide refuge
the sole private space we can steal
the one place I can be with you
where your other one just isn't real
I thought I could be stronger
but for affection I can't compete
I give up and say Uncle
back down and claim defeat
and abandon this illusion
pretending that we're real
stop this pain from compounding
allowing my heart to feel
now release my heart strings
and end your marionette show
I'll no longer perform for you
make your choice or let me go

Bling

Rubies crimson red, sapphires indigo blue
emeralds pure green, deep dark royal hue
amethysts of lavender, pearls translucent white
draped against my skin, triple strands my hearts delight
twenty-four carat diamonds blinded by their facets
stones of cut and quality enamoured of their assets
dripping head to toe in jewels glowing in their decadence
sparkle and glisten in the light shining with such radiance
but I would trade all these gems to be with you awhile
baubles pale in comparison to the brilliance of your smile
wrapped in your arms, your lips on mine are bliss
I'd be the richest girl from the golden wealth of your kiss

Green

Eyes as green as emeralds, like deep hypnotic seas
under spell in a trance, sending sparks through me
electricity coursing through my veins,
drowning in your eyes
running through their verdant meadows,
soaring their azure skies
emanating sunshine while planets orb around you
moon glowing in honour, why can't you see what I do?

Incarceration

Incarceration,
a cell from which I can't break free
if I could reduce my sentence
get out early on good behaviour
relegated to this solitary confinement
dreams of you slip like sand through my wanton fingers
while I sit in this hole and rot
melting away
all that's left now is sorrow
how I long to see
the stars twinkle in the sky,
the sun rise and fall on the horizon,
the moon's crazy effect on the tides
my senses starved,
my spirit held captive,
my soul lost,
a permanent resident in this purgatory of my making
with only room for memories of you
these prison bars are impenetrable
with iron shackles around my heart

Not Easy

Time and time again I've tried to hate you
even after all this time,
the years of hurt and pain,
disappointment and disillusion
but it still isn't easy to hate you
even after the incessant disrespect
and ill-mannered treatment
the taking advantage, all take and no give
treating me like a convenience
only when it suits you
why do you treat me this way time and time again?
even after multiple chances?
it's crazy to do the same thing over and over again
and expect a different result, then I must be crazy
crazy for falling,
crazy for staying,
crazy for loving,
and yet I still won't turn my back on you
when you come crying again
a case of amnesia may be my only salvation
to free my heart from your tight grip

Bloom

Once there was a garden
with hard, dry dirt
until one day
when I tilled the soil,
planted a seed,
watered it,
fed it,
nurtured it,
cared for it,
and watched it grow
soon the seed became a bud
then blossomed into a flower
now life blooms in my garden again
and you, the flower, give it life

Hunger

Electric emerald eyes smolder in the dark
a fire about to ignite friction causing spark
two voracious appetites starved for many days
only you satisfy my hunger with your lascivious ways
when you lift my mouth and press your lips to mine
I taste bourbon on your tongue so sweet and so sublime
ravish me with kisses, taste me with your lips
whisper words in my ear, leave me soaked in bliss
caress me soft and hold me, your touch I so adore
shaken not stirred, your soul leaves me wanting more

The Present

There once was a present
all wrapped up with care
with pretty pink ribbons
and a dash of flare

Then the package was placed
under the Christmas tree
so prominently displayed
for all to see

What I found in the box
not available in malls
there you were inside
the best present of all!!

Path

The path where you walked across my life
leaving a breadcrumb trail for me to follow
to a cabin in the woods far away from the world
with only room enough for our two hearts

Radiance

Even when you cannot speak
when no words will reach your lips
your exotic green eyes engage me
with a language only I can understand
it's all I'll ever need
without their radiance
my world would be dark

Blossom

Like a dahlia
blossoming from your light
absorbing your hearty soil
when you shine over me my petals open
spreading toward your sun

Lie

I could tell you that dark shadows
don't encompass my heart
that the sun rises and sets
and that stars twinkle in my sky
but it would be a lie
the sun has frozen
and planets stopped orbiting
since you went away

All That's Left

The sun sets
fizzling out like flat soda
the memory of your scent
and the touch of your skin
are all that's left
to keep me warm at night

Always

I know I've always loved you
even though we had never met
you were always there
waiting for me to notice
why did it took me so long
to see what was right there all along?

Bookends

You're the sentence to my words,
the predicate to my subject,
the adjective to my noun,
the exclamation point to my semi-colon,
the tome to my chapters
together we form a book
two bookends finding ourselves between sentences
a place where we can be and love
in those tender moments

Don't Want

I don't want to think
I don't want to be
no, not if you
can't be here with me
into the darkness
I slowly disappear
soon won't be able
to see nor to hear
unless you come back
to me for to stay
then together we'll be
forever our days

Once

Once upon a time
when there was love and you were mine
with days so happy and nights of bliss
your warm sweet mouth pressed on my lips
but life wasn't a fairy tale they just don't exist
evil is more than an ogre or witch
princes are rogues too busy to battle
for lovely fair maidens poisoned by apples
he's not looking for a princess but rather a toy
he's not a gentleman, he acts like a boy
he's no valiant knight he conquers and leaves
with just another notch etched on his sleeve
when the dream is over and I wake from sleep
Prince Charming's moved on with my heart to keep

Hands of Time

In a battle against the hands of time
I'm perpetually late
the pendulum swings
and the ticking grows ever louder
when the clock strikes midnight
I'm still on the dance floor
hoping for one more waltz
pining over a man who could only exist in a fairy tale
my coach long ago turned into a pumpkin
my prince now a warted frog
the moon turning its clockwork dream
time has all but run out
the ball has ended
and the glass slipper doesn't fit

Never Alone

When you feel you're all alone
fighting battles on your own
I'm always here even if we're apart
in my mind and especially my heart
whether in the dark or in the light
any time, both day or night
I'll share your joys and your sorrows
for today and all tomorrows

Wrapping

You stand behind me
wrapping me in your arms
planting soft kisses behind my ear
and down my neck
knowing it drives me wild
you always know how to press my buttons
and find the right spots

Same

The desire of your kisses
the feel of your tender touch
I long for you so much
I wonder if you feel the same

Lost in You

You're a constant presence on my mind
and all I want is to get lost in you

Home

Whatever I do, wherever I go
my heart beats inside of yours
no matter how much distance between us
home is wherever you are

Across the Horizon

You're not gone
you're a star in the sky
winking at me from above
as I await the moment
when you'll shoot across the horizon
landing safely in my arms

Shooting Star

You are a star
shooting across my sky
if I close my eyes
and make a wish
when you fall to earth
will you pick me up
and whisk me off with you
towards the infinite horizon?

Stranger

A stranger has taken residence in my head
its thoughts and feelings pushing mine out
to make room for its own
using my body as its host
losing myself to it in the process
a most unwelcome guest
unsatisfied until it's taken over
what once was me destroyed
now a stranger unto myself

Hope

What little hope was left has diminished
declining towards despair
in a place so dark and unbearable
please send me a sign

If Only

If only I could absorb your pain like a sponge
I would share your sorrow and lessen your burden
only you know the deafening volume
of the voices that torture your mind
the demons that took the beautiful smile
from your face and the joy from your eyes
no amount of tears I cry could ever match the river
that pours out from your soul

Unrequited

Like a storm he blew across my sky
carrying me like a weightless leaf
swirling and dancing in the air
powerless to fight the wind's vortex
then fall down to earth to be stepped on
and kicked aside
plucking daisy petals
he loves me, he loves me not
does he feel the same or am I a fool?
wanting something that may or may never be

Union

No formal dress
no fancy tux
just you, me and our love
it's all we've ever needed
a handful of daisies
a rose in your lapel
hand in hand
at a makeshift altar
professing our love
pronounced under the moon
and written in the stars
in a never-ending circle
placed around our fingers
and in our hearts

No Place I'd Rather Be

Paris,
London,
Madrid,
Rome

Greece,
Riviera,
Cabo,
home

There's no place I'd rather be
then wherever you are
no matter how near
no matter how far

Everything I need
is right here in your arms
when you look into my eyes
I submit to your charms

Crushed

I will stand again
my world doesn't revolve around you
while you tried time and time again
to knock me down
I was hurt but not crushed
don't give yourself credit
where it isn't due
I shall transcend and persevere
leaving you behind as dust in my wake

Match

You are the match that stokes my fire
please don't burn out

Serenity

Serenity washes over me
summoning me into a state of calm
my worries and cares dissipate
whenever you're around
an ever elusive peace
for a moment of time
comfort in your arms
solace now is mine

Inside of Me

You are the breath
breathing life inside of me
bringing meaning
back into my world
putting a skip back in my step
the colours you paint
on my monochrome canvas
reflect you like a prism
bursting in a rainbow
creating a light that shines
inside my heart and soul

Disappear

When you hold me
the whole world disappears
all that exists for me
is your arms and your breath
enveloping me in an ocean of love
with waves breaking gently over me
consuming me in your tide

Behind

Tried my best to ease the pain
the hurt you left behind
doing everything I can to forget you
but you're still on my mind

Loneliness

Counting hours of loneliness
sitting in the dark
melancholy days
meander away
aches my slow healing heart

Madness

Lost in a realm of madness
fallen through a crack
having no idea
how to find my way back
descending ever deeper
lost without a map
disoriented by a fog
in an all-encompassing trap

Winter

Trudging through the fallen snow
pure and crisp and white
cheeks all flushed and red
from cold wind and sunlight
holding hands, forging paths
leaving trails behind
across this winter wonderland
a world both yours and mine

Wilted Rose

Basking in your glow
a flower that once bloomed
now a wilted rose

My Garden

Overcome by weeds
will you tend to my garden
it needs your green thumb

Take Me

If you must go
if there's no choice but to die
then take me with you

Reach You

I'll trudge through deep snow
and walk over burning coals
so I can reach you

Absinthe

Absinthe green and smooth
exotic and forbidden
my favourite lady

All I See

Filled with endless doubt
of the talent inside you
yet that's all I see

Do Anything

I know now it's true
as long as you're beside me
I can do anything

Away

It hurts me to breathe
since the day you went away
my lungs deflated

Beacon

You are the sunlight
in my darkest nights
a welcome beacon

Body

The form of your body
makes me thirsty for water
desert oasis

Breath

The sound of your breath
as you sleep here beside me
soothes and comforts me

Radiant Sun

Enveloped in your warmth
kissed by your radiant sunlight
you brighten my life

Breath Away

Upon seeing you now
you take my breath away
like no one before

Occhi Verde

I tuoi occhi sono verde
come smeraldi trapassano
dentro a mia anima

Breathless

When I'm around you
I'm unable to focus
you leave me breathless

Grateful

I am so thankful
grateful for you in my life
for every moment

Way About You

Like no one else does
you have a way about you
that I love so much

I Am Nothing

Wind behind my sails
I am nothing without you
my inspiration

Butterflies

Butterflies inside me
I can hardly wait
to feel your touch

Anticipation

You move closer in
fingertips on my body
anticipation

Shower

My love showers you
kissing your every part
stroking your essence

Eternal Pain

It hurts me to breathe
since the day you went away
in eternal pain

Rare

Like a rare flower
your petals are fragile
needing special care

Never Far

You may be absent
but never far in my heart
I'll always love you

Pain

Such grief inside me
the pain in my soul comes through
now that you are gone

Canvas

My body's canvas
craves to be painted by you
in passion's colours

Magnet

She was drawn to him
like steel to a magnet
attracting her soul

Baited Breath

He speaks love to me
I listen with baited breath
hang on every word

Wish

If I had one wish
I would give up anything
for you in my arms

Without Reservation

I give you my heart
without reservation
to place inside yours

His Gaze

He could move planets
with the power of his gaze
in her direction
quickly captivating with
his gravitational pull

Where

Lead me to a place
where the night will never end
where the moon glistens
on passion's dewy-glowed skin
where love will last forever

Follow

I will follow you
whether you're near me or far
on roads high and low
doesn't matter where you are
I will always be with you

All Of Me

The total's more than the sum of its parts
with numerous scars and broken hearts
the good and the bad,
the happy and sad,
the whole and the damaged,
the pain and the ravaged
on a journey to repair me at last
from the ruin of others long past
a puzzle most incomplete
can you put together all of me?

Acknowledgments

I would like to thank my family, and Ben, my biggest supporter and the man who inspires me every day.

About the Author

L.M. Giannone is a writer of poetry, essays, and short stories. She's the author of three online series on Channillo.com: <u>No Vacancy</u>, a collection of humorous personal essays, <u>A Touch of Noir</u>, a collection of short stories written in *"noir"* style, and <u>All of Me</u>, a poetry series. She's currently scribing another poetry series, <u>Bits and Pieces</u>, on Wattpad. Her poems are also featured on Scriggler, Spillwords, and Niume. Three of her poems were published in the anthology <u>Poets Across Borders</u> available at amazon.co.uk. A new collection of poems and short stories will be released in spring 2017.

Readers can connect on Twitter (@LISAGNO), Instagram (@lmgiannoneauthor), wattpad.com/user/lmgiannone, or author site lmgiannone.com. The author can also be found on Goodreads and her Amazon Author Page.